For Ryan, Annabelle, Hope and Luke,
you are all gifts from God.
- B.B.R.

These are the gifts of the Holy Spirit,
wisdom, knowledge, understanding,
counsel, courage, reverence, awe and wonder.
Isaiah 11:2-3

Seven Gifts

Holy Spirit's powerful gifts for all children

Words and pictures by Barbara Brown Roessler

Library of Congress Control Number: 2018911699

ISBM: 978-0-692-18498-1 First Edition 2018

INSPIRED DESIGN PRESS
WWW.ROESSLERINSPIRED.COM

Copy Editor: Randal Roessler Cover design by b. roessler inspired design inc.
The illustrations in this book were done in mixed media. The text was set in Baskerville.

Acknowledgements

I'm so grateful to all my friends for their help and encouragement in the creation of this book. I'd especially like to thank
Bert Ghezzi, Susan Turo, Lauren B. Fournier, Kristie Altman, Jessica Sugiuchi and Peg Harding for being so generous
with their time and talents. Thanks also, to my dear friend and cheerleader, Liz Roehlk for always loving each new
revisions even more than the last. And I'm so very grateful for my husband Randy and all that he does to make my life
easier, and all that he's done to make SEVEN GIFTS possible.

Seven Gifts

Holy Spirit's powerful gifts for all children

Heavenly Father
sends these gifts to
help His children know,
how to have
a joyful heart where
love for Him
will grow.

The seven gifts are...

WISDOM

With
wisdom's grace
the heart
can learn,
to see
God's love
at every turn.

KNOWLEDGE

True knowledge
hopes each
child's aware
that
love from God
is love
to share.

UNDERSTANDING

When
understanding
fills the mind,
it lights
God's word
for faith
to find.

COUNSEL

Good counsel
guides
with loving care,
and
can be found
if asked
in prayer.

COURAGE

True courage
makes
the heart
grow strong,
and bold
to stand against
all wrong.

REVERENCE

Reverently
folded hands,
bowed head,
bring joy
and
love with
each prayer said.

AWE and WONDER

And wonder comes
with each new dawn,
each wave that breaks,
and then is gone.

So mighty
are His works, so broad,
that all creation bows to God!

All seven from
the Spirit,
the blessings each gift brings,
fill the heart
with gratitude,
and give the heart
its wings.

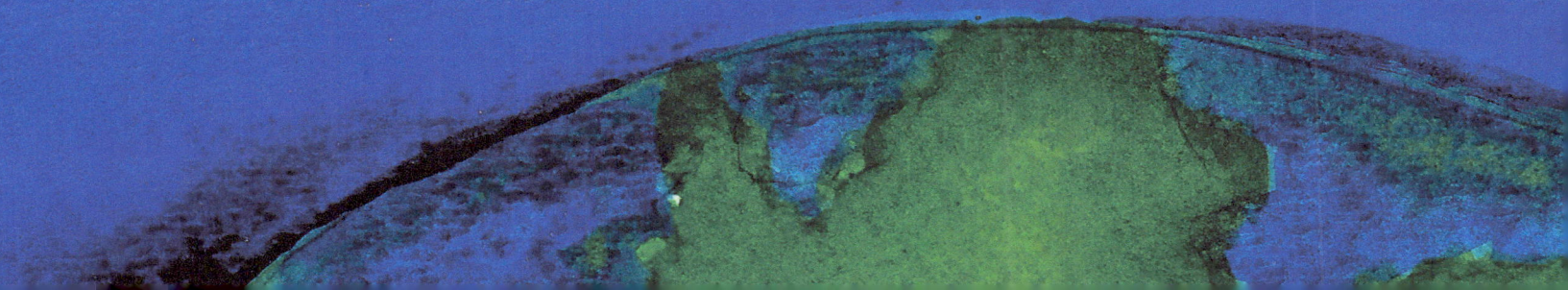